COMPUTERS

HISTORY OF SCIENCE

COMPUTERS

FROM BABBAGE
TO THE
FIFTH GENERATION

RON SCHNEIDERMAN

A GROLIER COMPANY

FRANKLIN WATTS
NEW YORK • LONDON • TORONTO
SYDNEY • 1986

Diagram by Vantage Art
Diagram and table from *Electronics:
The Continuing Revolution,* Abelson,
P. H. and Hammond, A. L., (eds.),
p. 44, AAAS.
Pub. No. 77-4, 1977.
Copyright 1986 by the AAAS.

Photographs courtesy of:
The Bettmann Archive: pp. 2, 4, 9, 10, 17, 27, 28;
IBM Archives: p. 20;
The Computer Museum, Boston, Massachusetts: p. 31
Sperry Corporation: p. 33;
A T & T Bell Laboratories: pp. 37, 38, 53;
Texas Instruments: p. 42.

Library of Congress Cataloging in Publication Data

Schneiderman, Ron.
Computers: from Babbage to the fifth generation.

(History of science)
Bibliography: p.
Includes index.
Summary: Traces the history of computers from the
earliest calculating machines to current stages of
development with artificial intelligence.
1. Computers—History—Juvenile literature.
2. Babbage, Charles, 1792-1871—Juvenile literature.
[1. Computers—History]   I. Title.   II. Series.
QA76.17.S36   1986   004   85-26316
ISBN 0-531-10131-2

CONTENTS

For my mother, who said:
"What do you mean, you wrote a book?
I sent you to summer camp and
you never even wrote me a letter."

CHAPTER

EARLY DEVELOPMENTS

In the earliest times, those who could count simply counted on their fingers. In fact, that's how 10 became the basis of the system of numbers that we use today. From there, people began using small rocks or pebbles to keep track of things. Then came notches or scratches on a wall or on a piece of wood to record and store information.

The first actual tool for calculating was probably the abacus. Developed by the Chinese about 5,000 years ago, it was made of wood and beads. It was actually the first hand-held calculator. So impressed with the abacus were travelers to China that its use began to spread and, in fact, it is still in use in some countries today. The abacus didn't actually do computing, of course, but it did help people keep track of numbers.

THE ARITHMETIC MACHINE

One of the earliest attempts to develop a calculator was in 1617 when John Napier, a Scottish mathematician, put together a set of rods made from bone or ivory. Each rod contained rows

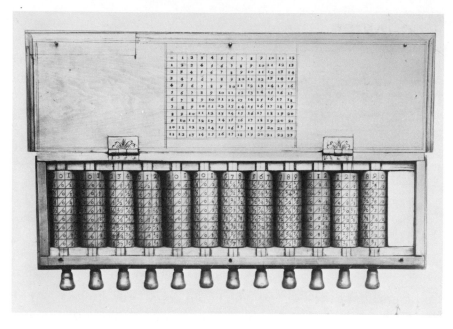

Scottish mathematician John Napier, inventor
of logarithms, devised a set of rods, later called
"Napier's Bones," for calculating numbers.

of numbers. By turning the rods, the numbers would add up by rows, showing the product of two large numbers.

Not too many years later, in 1642, a Frenchman named Blaise Pascal began to improve on Napier's idea of using rods to speed multiplication.

Pascal would have fit right in with today's young computer hackers. At age nineteen, Pascal went to work in his father's office, where his job was to add long columns of tax figures, a boring and time-consuming job. To make his job easier, he invented an Arithmetic Machine. The size of a shoe box, the machine not only could add and subtract, it could also convert sums of money between the different coinages of the time.

Pascal's Arithmetic Machine used notched wheels that moved each time a number was added or subtracted. It worked like an odometer in a car, which counts the number of miles traveled. The numbers 0 through 9 were printed on the edges of a row of wheels. The wheels were attached to each other, side by side. When a wheel made a complete turn from 0 to 9, a small notch made the next wheel move up one number. Others built calculating machines over the next fifty years, but they weren't much better than Pascal's Arithmetic Machine.

That changed in 1694 when a German mathematician, Baron Gottfried Wilhelm Leibnitz, demonstrated his Stepped Reckoner.

THE STEPPED RECKONER

The Stepped Reckoner could multiply and divide as well as add and subtract. Unlike Pascal's Arithmetic Machine, Leibnitz's invention had "stepped cylinders" rather than gears and wheels to do its calculations. Stepping was a new concept in calculators at the time. The idea was to break down a mathematical problem into small steps—so small that most humans would find making calculations in this manner very tedious. However, the Leibnitz machine was different from other new machines in the way it performed multiplication, which was by successive addition. In other words, to "multiply" 5 by 5 the Leibnitz machine would simply add the number five times.

Leibnitz actually got the idea for his machine twenty-three years earlier, in 1671, but he kept himself busy with other projects—some of them quite impressive. For example, he worked on the fundamental theories of calculus at about the same time as Sir Isaac Newton was working in the same field. By nature, Leibnitz was a hard worker. He worked constantly, seldom sleeping, sometimes working days at a time at his study armchair.

When he finally built the Reckoner, it didn't work very well. For one thing, it wasn't always accurate, mainly because it was

too complicated to be built with production methods that existed at the time. But even then, Leibnitz had a pretty good idea about the uses of his machine, predicting that it would be "desirable to all who are engaged in computations which, it is well known, are the managers of financial affairs, the administrators of others' estates, merchants, surveyors, geographers, navigators, astronomers, and those connected with any of the crafts that use mathematics."

JACQUARD'S LOOM

The first programmed machine was invented in 1801 by Joseph Marie Charles Jacquard, a French weaver. Jacquard wasn't thinking about computing, or even calculating, when he developed a new type of loom for weaving cloth.

The loom used punched cards to produce a variety of patterns. A needle with thread passed through a hole in a card. The process was repeated many times. Threads that could not pass through the card were not part of the pattern at that point. The weaving of a complete piece of material was controlled by a sequence of cards, forming the program for the process. The data that created the pattern were represented by the position of the holes in the cards. If, for example, the weaver wanted to repeat a pattern in a piece of material, he would use the same card or cards. The pattern would change when a new card was passed under the weaving needles with different colors of thread.

The original model of the loom constructed by French inventor Joseph Marie Jacquard. The loom used punched cards to produce a variety of patterns in cloth.

The loom caused problems in Jacquard's hometown of Lyons, France, where the old machine looms had been capable of weaving only plain cloth. Hand silk-weavers in the town began to fear that Jacquard's new loom would put them out of business. Ironically, many years later, in our own era, as computers became more of a fact of everyday life, many people expressed concern that this new mechanical marvel would eventually cause them to lose their jobs.

2

THE FIRST HARDWARE AND SOFTWARE

Charles Babbage's ideas were greeted with more enthusiasm than was Jacquard's loom. Born in Devonshire, England, in 1791, Babbage was the son of a merchant-banker. A pale and sickly child, he was educated mainly by private tutors until he went to Cambridge University. He was particularly good at math and would wake up early in the morning to study on his own. Babbage read every book on the subject that he could find. But there was still a great deal he didn't understand, and when he would ask his teachers about these things, he was often told that his questions were unimportant. It didn't take him long to figure out that he knew more about mathematics than his teachers did.

Babbage soon realized the shortcomings of trying to do large volumes of calculations with pen and paper. Although it was an accepted fact in his day that tables of calculations would be full of errors, it was unacceptable to him.

THE DIFFERENCE ENGINE

By 1812, when he was twenty, a frustrated Babbage started thinking seriously about the possibility of a mechanical calculating machine.

Sometime later, armed with many sketches he had made and some advice from a fellow student, John Herschel (who later became renowned as an astronomer), Babbage built a small model of what he called a Difference Engine. It was good enough, he thought, to warrant the building of a real machine.

In 1822, he proposed to the Royal Astronomical Society, which he had founded, the construction of a Difference Engine. Babbage's idea was for a machine that not only calculated, but also printed out the results. During this period, many ships were wrecked or lost because navigational tables were full of errors. Babbage pointed out that by calculating through the use of error-free tables in navigation, many ships would be saved from destruction. Thus, Babbage argued, the cost of developing his calculating machine would be justified. On the recommendation of the Royal Society, the chancellor of the Exchequer, the top treasury official in the English government, agreed to give Babbage 1,500 pounds to build the Difference Engine.

The original proposal was to build a machine that would produce tables quickly and accurately, but Babbage designed it to do other things too, such as solving equations. Unfortunately he seriously underestimated his task. His ideas and concepts were sound, but the technology didn't exist at that time to build a machine of the complexity and precision required to perform as Babbage envisioned. In fact. Babbage had to become his own toolmaker because the tools didn't exist to make the parts he needed for his machine. He struggled with the Difference Engine until 1833, constantly redesigning and rebuilding it. Finally, Babbage gave up on the project and turned his attention to another, even more advanced, idea—the Analytical Engine.

THE ANALYTICAL ENGINE

In the beginning, the Analytical Engine was to be fairly simple in design. It would calculate and tabulate to six decimal places. But as it began to take shape, problems arose, and as each prob-

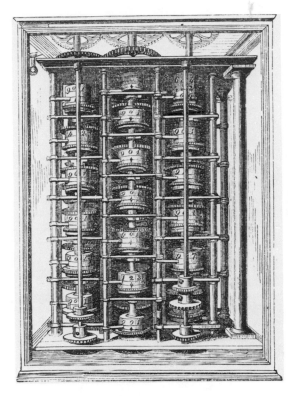

Charles Babbage labored for years to produce a machine that could calculate large numbers quickly and accurately. His Difference Engine was called "Babbage's Folly."

lem was overcome, Babbage came up with new ideas to make the machine better. Unfortunately, these ideas usually made it even more complex.

As Babbage described it, the Analytical Engine had two main parts. One was "the store [the computer's memory] in which all the variables to be operated upon, as well as those quantities which have arisen from the result of other operations, are placed." The second part, as Babbage explained it, was "the mill [what is today called the central processing unit, or CPU] into which the quantities about to be operated upon are always brought." Babbage also took a few ideas from Jacquard, using punched cards to "direct the nature of the operations to be performed."

His progress in developing the Analytical Engine was slowed because he also had a way of becoming distracted. Locks were a curiosity and he studied them well enough to write two pamphlets on them. He also invented a device that measured the vibration of buildings caused by traffic. And he took the time to write a book based on his study of mechanical devices and machinery in manufacturing as he designed and developed the Analytical Engine.

THE FIRST
COMPUTER PROGRAMMER

Babbage was a very sociable person and enjoyed being a part of his country's scientific community. He helped found a number of organizations dedicated to science and mathematics. At the Royal Astronomical Society, which he helped start with John Herschel in 1820, he met Lord Byron, the poet, and Byron's daughter, Ada Augusta King, Lady Lovelace. Lady Lovelace, it turned out, was a gifted mathematician. She not only understood Babbage's concepts, but was impressed by them. She volunteered to help him. In addition to introducing him to many influential people who could help finance Babbage's work, she also became deeply involved in the technical development of the Analytical Engine.

Like her father, Lady Lovelace was a talented writer. In 1843, she translated from French a technical paper written on the Analytical Engine, doing such a good job that Babbage encouraged her to add to the material. In the process, she not only expanded on Babbage's ideas with some of her own, but corrected errors in Babbage's work. The following year, the author

Ada Augusta King, Lady Lovelace, is
credited as the first computer programmer.

of the paper, who was a colleague of Babbage's, met Babbage's son, Herschel, and was surprised to learn from him that the notes added to his paper were done by Lady Lovelace and not by Babbage himself. She had signed them A. A. L. (Ada Augusta Lovelace), and he did not know of any English mathematician with those initials. Within a short time after the discovery of her achievement, mathematicians throughout Europe began to consider Lady Lovelace one of their own.

Lady Lovelace's major contribution to the Analytical Engine was her notion of repeating one set of instructions over and over when making a calculation. Today, these are usually called subroutines. Because of her work, Lady Lovelace is considered to be the world's first computer programmer.

THE LATER YEARS

Although distracted with other scientific projects, Babbage spent much of the period between 1848 and 1859 trying to raise enough money to finance construction of his engine. He tried several schemes, including investing in stock in the United States, but he lost most of his investment. He thought about writing a novel but never got around to it. He did write a few children's books, more for the fun of it than to raise money.

Lady Lovelace's life, meanwhile, was becoming more interesting, but also more complicated. She enjoyed the company of the top scientists of Europe. One of the men she met was Andrew Crosse, an inventor who specialized in the practical uses of electricity and magnetism. Crosse had a son, John, whom Lady Lovelace met and liked very much. John Crosse was a gambler; he particularly liked to bet on horse races. Lady Lovelace started betting on horses, and by 1848, she was seriously in debt.

Although she remained close to Babbage, Lady Lovelace maintained a relationship with John Crosse and continued to gamble. But in 1850, she discovered that she had cancer. Within two years, she was quite ill and even deeper in debt. Her mother helped her financially, but eventually even the family diamonds had to be pawned. While Lady Lovelace was bedridden and suffering, her mother dismissed her servants and would not allow Babbage to enter the house to visit. Ada Augusta King, Lady Lovelace, died at the age of thirty-six, the same age as her father when he died.

Babbage kept busy with his scientific activities and maintained a heavy social schedule, but he died in 1871 without completing his Analytical Engine. Indeed, he died thinking himself a failure.

THE LEGACY OF BABBAGE AND LADY LOVELACE

Babbage's youngest son, Henry Prevost Babbage, although without the brilliance of the father, continued construction of the mill section of the Analytical Engine. But he didn't get very far. Eventually, the mill, along with Babbage's notes and drawings, was placed in the Science Museum in London.

In 1879, a committee of the British Association for the Advancement of Science, another group which Charles Babbage helped organize, investigated the possibility of building an Analytical Engine. But because they were without any estimates of the cost of construction, and without Babbage's knowledge, they decided against it.

About ten years later, Henry decided to make another attempt at continuing his father's work. He designed a simple mill and had it built. The mill was able to compute a table of the first thirty-two multiples of π, but then it failed. It kept sticking, and no one, including Henry, could fix it. Henry gave up on the project and turned the mill over to the Science Museum.

Henry compiled much of his father's work, along with his own observations, into a book, *Babbage's Calculating Engines*. The book is probably the best source of information about Babbage's engines, and served as a reference for scientists and engineers well into the twentieth century.

Ada Augusta King, Lady Lovelace, hasn't been forgotten, either. The U.S. Department of Defense has recently adopted *Ada* as the name of its standard computer programming language.

HOLLERITH'S TABULATING MACHINE —AND IBM

Little changed in computer science over the next several years —until the U.S. Census Bureau decided that it needed a better and faster way to tabulate and sort information.

The first census of the United States was conducted in 1790. A census has been conducted every ten years since then. But by 1869, with over thirty-one million Americans to be counted, taking the census was becoming very complicated and expensive. And it took longer and longer to complete, as the population continued to grow. In fact, some feared that one census might not be completed before the next one was started.

A MOMENTOUS TRAIN TRIP

The problem of taking the census was eased somewhat with simple counting machines developed by Charles W. Seaton, then chief clerk of the census. But Seaton had a mining engineer working for him by the name of Herman Hollerith, who had some ideas about how to improve the census-taking. His first thought was to use punched cards. The idea didn't come from his knowledge of Jacquard's loom; rather, it came from a trip he remembered taking to the mines of Michigan. Hollerith had a train ticket with what was then called a punch photograph. The train conductor punched out a description of each passenger, marking the appropriate spot on the card where it indicated male or female, color of hair, and so forth.

Hollerith adopted that idea and designed cards that census-takers could carry around with them and punch in the field. They would then be processed by Hollerith's Tabulating Machine. The machine pushed pins against the cards. If a pin went through a hole, it would make contact with a metal plate under the card. The holes were placed carefully to indicate specific census information, such as age, gender, nationality, occupation, etc. When the pins made contact with the plate, it completed an electric circuit. That section of the machine was attached to a counter. The counter had four rows of ten clocklike dials. Each electric connection registered on the dial. Numbers could be carried from one dial to the next. All the machine operator had to do was keep feeding in punched cards and read the counts on the dials.

By 1889, Hollerith had three patents to his name. His machine was used in the 1890 census. Whereas the 1880 census had required close to eight years to tabulate, the 1890 census, using Hollerith's machine, was completed in only three years. It was so successful that Robert P. Porter, superintendent of the 1890 census, estimated that the machines saved the government about $5 million in labor costs.

THE FOUNDING OF IBM

Hollerith had become something of a celebrity; he was even awarded an honorary doctorate degree by Columbia University, where he had received his engineer of mines degree in 1879. Buoyed by his success at the Census Bureau, Hollerith decided to go into business.

Herman Hollerith's Tabulating Machine was first
used to take the United States census in 1890.
In this model the punched cards were fed into a
counter which registered the information on dials.
The cards were then deposited into a sorting box.

He formed the Tabulating Machine Company in 1896. It was probably the world's first computer company and, like many of the computer industry's entrepreneurs of today, he started making a lot of money almost immediately. He not only rented his machines for large fees to companies that found many different uses for them, but also sold thousands and thousands of punched cards, which could be used only once.

But by 1910, facing competition for the first time, Hollerith sold his company to Charles R. Flint, a banker-investor, who paid $450 for each share of the company. Hollerith received $1,210,500 for his shares and retired. Flint then merged the Tabulating Machine Company with other companies he owned: Computing Scale Company of Dayton, Ohio; the Bundy Manufacturing Company of Endicott, New York; and International Time Recording Company of Birmingham, New York. This new group of companies became known as Computing-Tabulating-Recording Company, or CTR.

In 1914, CTR hired Thomas Watson, a young salesman from the National Cash Register Company, as general manager. Watson took charge immediately and under his leadership, CTR grew rapidly. Hollerith died in 1929, but by then Watson had changed the name of CTR to International Business Machines—IBM. By 1939, IBM was the largest company in the field. Today, it is by far the largest computer company in the world, with annual revenues totaling well over $40 billion.

RESEARCH AT MIT

One of the first serious attempts to design a computer for use by scientists was made in 1930 by Vannevar Bush, the dean of engineering at the Massachusetts Institute of Technology (MIT) and a world-renowned scientist. He and a student, Harold Locke Hazen, built a machine out of electric motors, cranks, gears, and wires. It was an analog machine, measuring movement and distances and performing computations with these measurements. Bush called the machine a Differential Analyzer.

In 1935, Bush tried to improve on his work with a second machine, which used electrical rather than mechanical devices. But even that effort was outdated as soon as the machine was built; as other scientists and engineers were already looking at electronics to handle mathematical computations. They began designing circuitry for automatic calculating machines. It wasn't long before the Differential Analyzer ended up in the Smithsonian Institution, along with so many other scientific curiosities in history.

THE UNIVERSAL CALCULATOR

The next serious attempt at developing a calculator/computer was a joint venture of Harvard University and IBM. The project got its start when Howard H. Aiken, a Harvard engineer, wrote a paper that described the need for a machine that would perform complete calculations entirely automatically. When it was finally built in 1944, the IBM Automatic-Sequence-Controlled Calculator, or Mark I, as it was called, was huge. It measured 51 feet (15.5 m) long and was 8 feet (2 m) high, with close to 800,000 components, some of them taken from existing IBM machines. It was considered fast at the time—able to add and subtract two twenty-three-digit numbers in three-tenths of a second.

Completed in 1944, the giant calculator embodied many of the concepts of the Babbage machine. But there were significant improvements. For example, programs were punched on paper tape rather than individual cards, making it unnecessary to give the machine each instruction as it was being executed, which was necessary with Jacquard's loom and the machine Babbage had in mind.

The Harvard/IBM machine later became known as the Mark I.

The Mark I, built in 1944, embodied many of Babbage's concepts. The fastest calculator at the time, it could add and subtract two twenty-three-digit numbers in three-tenths of a second.

This is because Aiken had set up a laboratory at Harvard to build improved versions of the first machine for the U.S. Navy, Air Force, and Army. These newer machines were named Mark II, Mark III, and Mark IV. Although the Harvard/IBM machine is often referred to as a computer, and it did, in fact, perform logical operations, most scientists of the time preferred to call it a universal calculator. In any case, it led the way to the development of the first all-electronic digital computer.

CHAPTER

FIRST GENERATION COMPUTERS— BIG AND SLOW, BUT ELECTRONIC

While most scientists and engineers continued to struggle with electromechanical computers, others were beginning to think electronics. One was Dr. John Vincent Atanasoff, a mathematician and physicist at Iowa State University. In 1939, Atanasoff and one of his students, Clifford Berry, built a working model of a small computer that did arithmetic electronically. But it was more of a calculator than a computer. To make it a computer, Atanosoff and Berry used electrical capacitors, which could hold an electrical charge to store numbers. The capacitors were mounted on two drums made of Bakelite, a plastic material prepared by heating certain chemicals under pressure. Each drum could store thirty binary numbers of fifty binary digits (bits) each. (A binary number system is based on two numbers, 0 and 1.) The numbers could be read as the drums were rotated. The computer could add and subtract. It had no mechanical parts; everything was electronic.

But Atanosoff and Berry never put the finishing touches on their computer—it was never a complete working model—and they stopped work on it to turn their attention to scientific projects related to World War II.

Late in 1940, Atanasoff attended the annual meeting of the American Association for the Advancement of Science in Philadelphia. One of the speakers at that meeting was Dr. John W. Mauchly, then head of the physics department at Ursinus College, not far from Philadelphia. Mauchly had long been interested in improving the speed of calculating machines, and talked about using computing machines to help analyze statistical information to improve weather forecasting.

After Mauchly's speech at the conference, Atanasoff introduced himself and mentioned his interest in computing. Later, at Atanasoff's invitation, Mauchly visited him in Iowa. What was planned as a short visit stretched into several days while the two scientists traded information and shared their ideas about computing.

Mauchly knew that physicists were already experimenting with vacuum tubes to count and analyze cosmic rays. By the time he met Atanasoff, he had already begun to assemble some equipment in the lab at Ursinus, using neon tubes. They weren't as good as vacuum tubes, but they were cheaper. Mauchly had to pay for everything out of his own pocket; the school's budget was too small for new projects. Mauchly's personal budget was also small—his teaching salary was $1,500 a year, which was less than many unskilled workers earned at the time.

HELPING WIN THE WAR

To further his knowledge of the new art of electronics, Mauchly began taking summer school courses at the Moore School of Electrical Engineering at the University of Pennsylvania in Philadelphia. The courses were financed by the U.S. Army's Ballistic Research Laboratory in Aberdeen, Maryland, which, during World War II, wanted to train people to help improve its artillery calculations. At that time, it took one person using a desk calculator three weeks to produce a single artillery trajectory (the path of a shell). Since there were thousands of possible trajectories in aiming a gun, and different kinds of ammunition, the

Army lab employed hundreds of people to do this work. But the workload grew, and they kept falling behind.

That would soon change. At the Moore School, Mauchly met J. Presper Eckert, who had just received his bachelor's degree in electrical engineering. Eckert had become a lab instructor in the course. When Mauchly discovered that Eckert had a special interest in improving the reliability of vacuum tubes, he suggested they work together to develop an electronic calculator.

Their work became known to Army Lieutenant Herman Goldstine. Goldstine played a major role in helping the university win a contract from the Army to develop and build the first electronic computer. In fact, Goldstine became so involved in their research that he got the Army to transfer him from the Aberdeen lab to the Moore School.

They called this machine the Electronic Numerical Integrator and Computer (ENIAC). The Army colonel who approved the project added the words "and Computer" to the title originally selected for the machine. That was in 1943.

A GIANT CALLED ENIAC

During the development stage, Mauchly concentrated on defining what functions the computer should perform and what equipment or components would be needed to handle those functions. Eckert was responsible for determining what they would actually build. They worked very closely and very carefully during the eighteen months it took to build ENIAC—designing and testing everything along the way.

Even though they started with existing materials and components, such as vacuum tubes, Mauchly and Eckert performed a tremendous amount of original research in developing ENIAC. At one point, for example, they had to build twenty accumulators as part of the computer. These were storage devices that temporarily retained numbers (arithmetic solutions, indexes, or operation instructions) in the processor. Each accumulator had ten decade counters, and each counter contained ten "flip-flop" devices, which can count either the presence or absence of electric current. Every accumulator could store a ten-digit number. The accumulators were paired to handle a twenty-digit number if necessary. Although only a part of the ENIAC, the accumulators consisted of several hundred tubes in a panel 2 feet (61 cm) wide and about 8 feet (2 m) high.

Component reliability was extremely important, because with 18,000 vacuum tubes in the computer, a lot could go wrong. Before assembling the entire system, Mauchly and Eckert first built a two-accumulator model and tested it. That turned out to be a good move, because even though it worked the first time they tried it, they realized it could be improved and they reworked the design. They also built a high-speed multiplication unit because they knew multiplication would be an important function in artillery and general-purpose computations. Eckert also devised new techniques for using vacuum tubes, based on methods already developed with cosmic rays in nuclear-physics laboratories.

They considered magnetic recording for data storage but didn't have time to develop that method because the Army wanted the computer as soon as it could get it. In the interest of time, ENIAC's inputs and outputs were handled by a method first used many years earlier—punched card.

When completed, ENIAC weighed 30 tons (27 mt), covered about 1,500 square feet (140 sq m) of floor space (about the size of a small house), and required 160 kilowatts of power—enough to heat a sizable building. At its official dedication in February 1946, ENIAC demonstrated successfully its ability to calculate an artillery trajectory. The computer program for the demonstration was written by Herman Goldstine's wife, Adele.

MAINFRAMES

Shortly after the war, the president of the University of Pennsylvania signed a letter to the co-inventors giving them full rights

The first electronic computer was the ENIAC, developed in 1946 for military purposes.

Hungary's John von Neumann conceived the idea of storing programs in the computer's memory, eliminating the necessity of a human operator performing numerous time-consuming steps manually. He is shown (right) standing with American physicist Robert Oppenheimer in front of the EDVAC computer, completed in 1950.

to the ENIAC. But in 1947, a university administrator who had returned from the war demanded that Mauchly and Eckert return the rights to the school. They refused and then left the university to form their own company, Electronic Control Company, later changing the name to Eckert-Mauchly Computer Corporation.

Mauchly and Eckert tried to convince bankers and Wall Street financiers that they should invest in the development of a commercial computer. They didn't believe it would be a big problem because the future of computers seemed so obvious to them. They were wrong. The financial people couldn't see how something with 18,000 tubes, that cost $500,000, and that was so costly to operate could ever become practical. In fact, the electric bill to run ENIAC in 1946 was $1,800 a month—quite a bit considering that workers in the United States earned an average of $45.58 a week at that time.

Still, Mauchly and Eckert pushed ahead. With some financial backing from the U.S. Census Bureau, which needed help in computing its data, they built their second digital computer, BINAC, and started work on UNIVAC I, the first large commercial computer.

Their company was acquired by Remington Rand in 1950, and Mauchly headed that company's Univac Applications Research Center until 1959. While at Univac, he finally realized part of his dream to use computers in weather forecasting, proving from weather statistics that the probability for large amounts of rainfall is highest right after a full or new moon.

THE COMPUTER
ACQUIRES MEMORY

Over the next several years, a number of people would play very important roles in the development of the computer industry. One was John von Neumann. As a six-year-old in his native Budapest, von Neumann could, among other feats, divide two eight-digit numbers in his head. He earned a doctoral degree at the age of twenty-two. After teaching for a short time at the University of Berlin in Germany, von Neumann joined the faculty of the Institute for Advanced Study at Princeton University. He had so many ideas and worked on so many projects at one time, that he allowed himself only five hours sleep a night.

Shortly after the ENIAC was built, von Neumann came up with an idea that changed computer designs forever. ENIAC required a human operator to plug in hundreds of wires to connect one part of the machine with another. The way the wires were plugged in determined what operations the machine would perform. In von Neumann's design, instructions that tell the computer what to do with the data could be stored in the computer's memory, doing away with ENIAC's plugboard method. Most computers in use today are designed around von Neumann's idea of storing programs in memory.

"ON COMPUTABLE NUMBERS"

One of the most important figures in the development of the computer, and one who has become almost lost in the history of computer technology, is Alan M. Turing. An English mathematician, Turing wrote a paper, "On Computable Numbers," in 1937, in which he described a machine that, with the proper instructions, and using punched paper tape to control its operations, would imitate any other machine. That highly technical paper, dealing with the most advanced mathematical theories, developed several significant conclusions that proved to be a major contribution to the future of computer design.

Turing's career as a mathematician and computer scientist was interrupted by World War II. Prior to the war, he had studied codes and ciphers as a hobby. With that experience, plus his mathematical knowledge, Turing played an important role in breaking the codes of the German cipher machine, the Enigma,

Alan Turing's mathematical genius was demonstrated during World War II when he succeeded in breaking the codes of the Enigma, the German cipher machine.

and helping Britain obtain information on the location and battle capabilities of German submarines.

Following the war, Turing worked at the British National Physical Laboratory on the development of an electronic computer called the Automatic Computing Engine (ACE). In its design, emphasis was placed on a large and fast electronic memory. In addition to his computer design and development efforts, Turing also gave thought to how a general-purpose computer could be used. The ACE, he wrote in a report, would handle "problems which can be solved by human clerical labor, working to fixed rules," just as most computers do today.

ACE required only 2,000 vacuum tubes, compared with 18,000 for Mauchly and Eckert's ENIAC, and had a memory capacity of 6,000 numbers compared with 20 numbers for the ENIAC. But the ENIAC was built and put into useful operation first and got most of the attention. The first ACE wasn't built until 1946 and that was a demonstration model.

Another version, called DEUCE, was built later for commercial use. Both were sent to the Science Museum in London in 1958 when the National Physical Laboratory produced a larger machine, also called ACE. That unit contained much of the technology suggested by Turing in his original designs, but it was built four years after Turing's death. By that time, American computer scientists were already using transistors instead of vacuum tubes and other advanced designs that made the ACE seem like an antique.

COBOL

Another major contributor to the early development of the digital electronic computer was Grace Murray Hopper, who worked for Mauchly from 1949 to 1959, during the period when UNIVAC I was being built.

After receiving M.A. and Ph.D. degrees, Grace Hopper taught mathematics from 1931 to 1942. In 1943, she entered the

Grace Hopper, the creator of COBOL, wrote the first programs that would translate English into binary numbers.

U.S. Naval Reserve as a lieutenant. Assigned to the Bureau of Ordnance Computation Project at Harvard University, she programmed the Mark I computer. In fact, some historians credit her with actually saving the Mark I by writing the highly complex instructions that made it work.

Rather than starting from scratch with every single program, Grace Hopper created a computer language that programmers could learn and use over and over. Called COBOL (for Common Business-Oriented Language), it remains the most common language used in large business computer systems today.

In 1946, she joined the Harvard faculty as a research specialist in computation and continued work on the Mark II and Mark III computers for the Navy. In 1952, Grace Hopper wrote the first programs that would translate English into binary numbers, called compiler programs. Without compilers, programmers would have to write software in complicated, so-called machine language—a time-consuming and unproductive method of program development.

Promoted to commodore in 1983, at the age of seventy-seven, Grace Hopper continues to serve on active duty at the Naval Data Automation Command in Washington, D.C. She is the Navy's oldest officer on active duty.

CHAPTER

TRANSISTORS AND THE SECOND GENERATION

Second generation computers didn't begin to emerge until 1959. But there may not have been a second generation without the development of the transistor in the late 1940s.

The transistor didn't just happen. It wasn't an accidental discovery, but was the result of a highly organized research effort at the Bell Telephone Laboratories in New Jersey, an effort aimed at finding a solid-state amplifier and switch to replace the vacuum tube.

Prior to World War II, Dr. Melvin J. Kelly, director of research at Bell Labs, became concerned about the limitations of the vacuum tube in the telephone industry. He knew that within ten to fifteen years, the telephone company would have to process more and more information—very quickly, reliably, and cheaply. Vacuum tubes were too big, consumed too much power, were expensive to manufacture, and they didn't last very long. Mechanical relays, which were a possible alternative to tubes, although inexpensive, operated slowly and took up too much space.

They had to try something new. The most promising possibility at the time seemed to be semiconductors—materials whose electrical conductivity is between that of a conductor and an insulator. Bell Labs decided to explore the behavior of electronics in these solid materials.

World War II interrupted most of the work. But the war stimulated research in certain materials needed for the war effort, such as silicon and germanium detectors for radar, and the understanding of these two semiconductors contributed to the invention of the transistor.

A PRIZE-WINNING TEAM

In 1945, Kelly authorized a major effort in solid-state research. The team's primary researchers were physicists Dr. William Shockley, who had joined Bell Labs in 1936; Dr. John Bardeen, who joined the Labs late in 1945, just in time to take part in the project; and Dr. Walter Brattain, a member of the Labs' staff since 1929.

Their goal was to produce a device that would perform better than the vacuum tube. Experiments led to new theories. One member of the research team would make a proposal and, when it didn't quite work out as expected, another member would make suggestions for improvements.

On December 23, 1947, Bardeen and Brattain demonstrated a device that amplified a speech signal twenty times. It was called a point-contact transistor because it consisted of two pointed gold contacts, less than two-thousandths of an inch apart, on one side of a piece of material called a germanium wafer.

The word *transistor* was actually coined by Dr. John R. Pierce, who was executive director of research at Bell Labs' Communications Sciences Division. He came up with the word as a contraction of "transfer resistor," which describes the transistor's electrical behavior. Electrical pathways in these semiconductors had "switches" which would transfer or resist the passage of electricity.

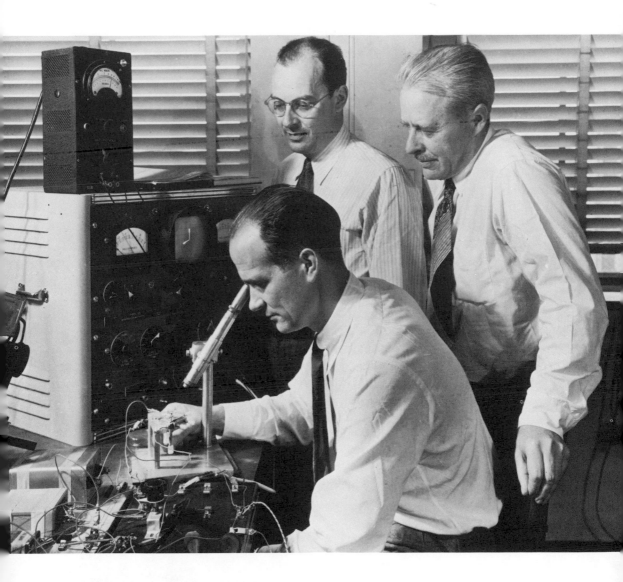

*Shown here are William Shockley (seated),
John Bardeen (standing left), and Walter
Brattain, working on the first transistor.*

BELL'S TRANSISTOR

Officially, December 23, 1947, is considered the date the transistor was "invented." But the junction transistor, a device made of silicon, which is used in most electronic circuits today, was conceived by Shockley exactly a month later—on January 23, 1948. This transistor did just about everything the three scientists had set out for it to do—it was faster, cheaper, generated a lot less heat, required less space, and was more reliable than vacuum tubes.

The invention of the transistor was announced on June 30, 1948, at a press conference in New York City. A news release issued that day, stated:

> An amazingly simple device, capable of performing efficiently nearly all the functions of an ordinary vacuum tube, was demonstrated for the first time yesterday at Bell Telephone Laboratories, where it was invented. . . . Bell scientists and engineers expect it may have far-reaching significance in electronics and electrical communications.

The announcement didn't attract much attention. The New York Times gave it four column-inches on its radio and movie page. The transistor received much greater coverage in 1956 when Bardeen, Brattain, and Shockley were awarded the Nobel Prize in physics for their work on the transistor.

This first transistor amplified electrical signals by passing them through a solid semiconductor material. It revolutionized the electronics industry.

The impact of the transistor has been enormous. Originally developed as a solid-state replacement for vacuum tubes in telephone equipment, the transistor can now be found everywhere—in digital watches, home appliances, calculators, radios and television, and, of course, computers.

We would never have gone to the moon without the invention of the transistor. Today, every industry and its products, including the automobile, musical instruments, medicine, and communications, just to name a few, have been affected by the transistor.

CHAPTER

THIRD-GENERATION
INTEGRATED
CIRCUITS—
AND THE FOURTH

Scientists and engineers working in the semiconductor and computer industries have managed, over the years, to make things better—enhancing and improving their designs and products. Occasionally, as in the case of the transistor, there is a major breakthrough that changes the industry. The integrated circuit, or IC, was such a development.

In 1957, Dr. Robert Noyce and seven co-workers decided to leave Shockley Semiconductor Laboratories, formed earlier by William Shockley shortly after he left Bell Labs. They formed their own company with financial backing from Fairchild Camera & Instrument Company. At Fairchild Semiconductor Corporation, the new company, Noyce began thinking about integrating various electronic functions, such as capacitors, transistors, diodes, and resistors, on a single slice, or chip, of silicon.

At about the same time, in 1958, Jack St. Clair Kilby, an electrical engineer, joined Texas Instruments Inc. in Dallas. His first assignment was to design a device for the army called a "micromodule." It was a circuit in which components of the same size could be snapped together like a plastic puzzle without special electrical wiring. A few months later, while every-

Jack Kilby's original integrated circuit. It contained, within a single semiconductor crystal, the equivalent of five electronic devices: one transistor, three resistors, and one capacitor.

one at Texas Instruments was taking a required two-week July vacation, Kilby, who hadn't been at the company long enough to earn vacation time, was left alone in the lab. It struck him that since silicon can be used as the raw material for most basic electronic components, it might be possible to put all the components in a single block of material without actually wiring anything together. The device that he envisioned came to be known as an integrated circuit.

Almost all by itself, the IC created the third-generation of computers. It was ten times faster than the transistor and became the basis for most of the developments in computer technology today.

So significant is Kilby's integrated circuit that his portrait hangs in Washington in the National Inventor's Hall of Fame, between Henry Ford and Ernest O. Lawrence, the inventor of the atom smasher.

REFINING THE INTEGRATED CIRCUIT

Noyce improved on Kilby's IC design almost immediately, developing a "planar process," which electrically separated circuit elements by inserting an insulated layer across the surface of the silicon chip rather than by cutting them apart and wiring them together again.

Since then, the technology has moved along quickly, with many improvements being made by others. By 1963, ICs represented about 10 percent of the total number of electronic circuits produced in the United States. Although the size of the chips themselves remains about the same, the number of individual circuits that can be placed on a chip is doubled every year.

THE FOURTH GENERATION

Noyce left Fairchild in 1968 to form his own company, Intel Corporation. One of the company's first jobs was assigned to Ted Hoff, an Intel engineer. Hoff was given the task of designing a new calculator with integrated circuits for a Japanese desktop calculator manufacturer. In order to keep the device small enough to fit on a desk, Hoff jammed all of the calculator's arithmetic and logic functions onto the same chip. The remaining circuitry was designed to fit onto two additional chips. But the first, and most important, development was Hoff's integrated chip. It was the first time a complete central processing unit was placed on a single chip. Intel called it a microprocessor. But it soon became more popularly called a computer-on-a-chip. (The advantages of the microprocessor over the lumbering ENIAC are evident in the table on page 44.)

Comparison of parameters of ENIAC with the Fairchild 8 (F8) microprocessor.
Abbreviations: CPU, central processing unit; TTY, teletype terminal; ROM, read only memory; RAM, random access memory.

Item	Parameter	ENIAC	F8*	Comments
1	Size	3,000 cubic feet	0.011 cubic feet	300,000 times smaller
2	Power consumption	140 kilowatts	2.5 watts	56,000 times less power
3	ROM	16K bits (relays and switches)	16K bits	Equal amount
4	RAM	1K bits (flip-flop accumulators)	8K bits	Eight times more RAM in F8
5	Clock rate	100 kilohertz	2 megahertz	20 times faster clock rate with F8
6	Transistors or tubes	18,000 tubes	20,000 transistors	About the same
7	Resistors	70,000	None	F8 uses active devices as resistors
8	Capacitors	10,000	2	5,000 times less
9	Relays and switches	7,500	None	
10	Add time	200 μsec (12 digits)	150 μsec (8 digits)	About the same
11	Mean time to failure	Hours	Years	More than 10,000 times as reliable
12	Weight	30 tons	< 1 pound	

Add a keyboard to the microprocessor for input, a video display to read the computer's output, a storage device (such as a floppy disk drive), and the result is a fourth-generation-computer—able to perform over 10 million calculations a second, which is ten times faster than third-generation computers.

Today, millions of people have personal computers on their office desks and in their homes. The technology in personal computers, or microcomputers, is advancing rapidly with improvements being made constantly. Computers are getting faster, they are able to store more data, and they are available with lots of new accessories and software that make them easier to use. But it's only the beginning of some real excitement in what has become known as the Information Age.

7

ARTIFICIAL INTELLIGENCE AND THE FIFTH GENERATION

Where do we go from here? What's next? Under development are computers that will serve as our ears, eyes, mouth, and brain—computers that can understand natural human language, recognize objects, learn, infer, reason, and solve problems as humans do. They do this by inference—by drawing conclusions rather than by numeric calculations. What we used to call an "electronic brain" in science fiction stories and movies is no longer fiction. Engineers and scientists today are developing computers that use human knowledge as basic units to be processed—in essence, machines that think. It is the beginning of the fifth generation.

COMPUTERS THAT CAN THINK

One very important part of this development Is artificial intelligence, or AI. In computer terms, AI simulates human intelligence. Using AI techniques, computers can communicate with humans in natural language. They can learn, make deductions (what computer scientists call inference), and even make decisions.

AI started to get some attention at a two-month summer conference at Dartmouth, New Hampshire, in 1956. At that time, a group of scientists met to explore ways to make computers act or "think" like humans. The conference was organized by John McCarthy, at the time an assistant professor of mathematics at Dartmouth College. At the conference, Logic Theorist, a computer program that used the first symbolic processing language, IPL (Information Processing Language) was presented for the first time to the AI researchers. It was developed by Allen Newell and Herbert Simon of Carnegie Institute of Technology in Pittsburgh (now Carnegie-Mellon University), along with J. C. Shaw of the Rand Corporation, an independent research organization in Santa Monica, California.

Logic Theorist used a computer as a symbolic, in addition to a numeric, processor. Programs such as BASIC and FORTRAN represent and manipulate data as numbers. AI languages are designed to handle nonnumerical symbols as well, such as words, phrases, or geometric shapes. In symbolic processing, programmers can link these symbols, or objects, in ways that are similar to the way the human brain stores and structures knowledge. These symbolic elements are eventually translated by a language interpreter into binary numbers, or "machine" language—the only language that computers can actually understand. In fact, AI research probably came along when it did because programmers wanted the ability to create pictorial information with their computers. Their first attempts at producing computer graphic software programs weren't very good, but they were the start of some very important work that now allows the creation of charts and graphs for use in business, two-dimensional and three-dimensional drawings for scientific and engineering design projects, and even graphic programs for computer games.

By the late 1950s, McCarthy had developed LISP (List Processing Language), to write AI programs. It is, to this day, the most popular AI computer language.

EXPERT SYSTEMS

Today, after thirty years of research and development by scientists and engineers in both universities and industry, AI programs are beginning to find practical uses. Most of these AI programs are called knowledge-based or "expert" systems. Expert systems help solve problems in specialized areas that normally would require an expert. The knowledge base is the information that the expert system can draw from, such as that supplied by engineers, scientists, doctors, and other specialists. These systems are already being used today in such areas as medical diagnostics to help doctors make decisions on patient care, and by oil companies to predict what, if any, valuable minerals might be found at a geological site. Also, expert systems are used to help develop financial information for bankers and other specialists. Eventually, home computer users will use knowledge-based expert systems to tell them what is wrong with their car or home appliance, and how to fix it.

An expert system would come in handy if, for example, you were in charge of an oil drilling rig team in a remote desert location. Because of the area, the heavy equipment involved, and the number of skilled people on the job, drilling for oil is a very expensive operation. Suppose that the drill, which is now deep in the ground, gets stuck. It won't move—up or down. This is not an uncommon problem, but there are only a few people in the world—experts—who know how to unstick an oil drill. And you can't locate any of them.

Fortunately, you have anticipated the problem with an expert system developed just for this purpose. You can sit down at a computer or call someone with access to the program, and it will take you through a series of questions. For example: How deep is the drill bit? What type of bit is in use? What kind of material is it stuck in? The questions get more detailed and more technical. Even if you're not sure of the answer, you can take a good guess, just as the experts might do if they were there with you. After you have run through the entire series of questions, the program will not only tell you what it believes to be the problem, it will suggest what to do about it.

Expert systems are also being used in hospitals. After accepting a patient's test results, the system asks questions. From this information, the system can identify the patient's malady and recommend a course of treatment.

Another expert system is used to repair trains. Maintenance crews type in responses to questions about the train's malfunction described on the computer screen. From that information, the system not only identifies the cause of the malfunction, but also displays the problem graphically and shows how to make the repair. If needed, detailed drawings of the locomotive's various parts and how they work together can be displayed on the screen.

Expert systems are becoming so sophisticated that they soon may actually make decisions for us, based on the knowledge stored in the computer's memory. For example, how should you invest your money? Expert systems have been written, based on the knowledge of experts, that tell you how to do that.

One of the things that scientists like about expert systems is that they're more consistent than people. As long as you give the same set of answers, you get the same responses. However, people are always learning and gaining experience, and expert systems don't learn. Also, even human experts, with the same education and experience, may have different opinions about how to deal with a problem. Future expert systems will solve these problems. These newer systems will gain knowledge by "reading" technical and even general interest information. They could, for example, read the latest developments in medical books and other sources to learn the latest techniques for treating diseases and the newest surgical procedures.

COMPUTERS THAT UNDERSTAND ENGLISH

The use of natural language will also become an important part of AI. Someday you will be able to enter a command into a computer in English—in your own words. Once the computer understands the command, it will display the information requested.

Computer programs that understand requests phrased in English are quite different from conventional computer programs. For example, conventional computer languages define in advance a set of commands that the system will execute. These commands are the only instructions the system will understand. But if the computer program is designed for natural language, you can phrase your request any way you want. Only the proper use of English is required. But the system understands these commands only if they are entered according to certain rules.

Any good natural language must be able to handle four key elements. No system can be expected to understand all of the English language. But the system should be able to deal with enough of the language to make it useful. And it must be able to handle small changes in the wording of a request, since you may not remember exactly the same words every time you make a similar request.

A second important element is in the language itself. When you ask someone a question, it may be interpreted in different ways. Part of the problem a computer has in dealing with this is in the fact that some words have different meanings. A good example is the word *baker.* If you typed that word into the computer, the system might not be able to figure out if it was someone's last name or someone's occupation.

A natural language must also be able to retrieve data from several files to answer a request. To do this, it must know how to instruct the database (that portion of the system with all the information) to relate, or join, files to answer a question.

Finally, natural language programs should be able to handle both factual and projected information, such as a company's actual sales, as well as its estimated sales for any period of time.

AI techniques are only now beginning to be used in business and industry, and in science and engineering. Much research and development remains to be done before additional practical uses are found for this technology. There are plenty of ideas, however. One useful application would be the ability to translate languages from, say, Chinese to English. Another possibility for the future is the development of programs that would understand poorly written articles and edit them. The most important efforts in AI, currently under way, will help us better understand how to manage larger and more complex collections of knowledge and information.

SUPERCHIPS AND SUPERCOMPUTERS— FASTER AND CHEAPER

Within about ten years, microprocessors—computers on a chip, which provide the processing power in most personal computer systems—will be ten to fifteen times faster than they are today. And they will probably be cheaper.

The use of microprocessors is growing constantly. They cost only a few dollars apiece, but total sales of these devices are expected to reach $4.5 billion by 1989, or about four times 1984 sales levels. Microprocessors are being used not only in computers, but in many everyday consumer products, such as automobiles, fire alarms, cameras, office copying machines, videocassette recorders, microwave ovens, washing machines, and

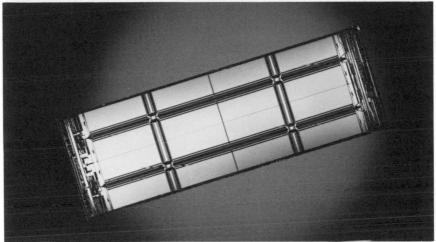

Above: a close-up view of a microprocessor.
Not visible because of their 1.75-micro-
meter size are its 180,000 transistors.
Below: the megabit computer memory
chip, smaller than a dime, can store over
one million digital bits of information.

small electrical appliances. With so much interest in microprocessors, manufacturers are developing faster and more powerful chips—superchips.

Texas Instruments is designing and building a LISP central processing unit—an AI processor on a single chip. The chip will have between 600,000 and 700,000 transistors, which is roughly ten times the number of transistors in the Motorola 68000, one of the most widely used microprocessors today. When developed, the TI chip will make it possible to design a LISP computer system the size of a shoe box. But what's really exciting to its developers is that it may make symbolic processing available to a more general audience in the same way that microprocessors have made personal computers possible. In other words, everyone will be able to use artificial intelligence systems, not just trained computer scientists.

Another company, Proximity Technology Inc., based in Florida, has developed a chip that can find similarities between strings of characters. Today's computers have problems with simple spelling errors in instructions. Proximity's "intelligent" chip will recognize the problem and figure out what a misspelled word really means.

Also, NCR Corporation has introduced a chip designed for processing and analyzing images. It will, for example, allow robots to "see."

SMART COMPUTERS
FOR DEFENSE

Researchers at AT&T Bell Laboratories are working on a "ballistic transistor" that switches at ten femtoseconds (a femtosecond is one quadrillionth of a second). Eventually, transistors operating at these speeds will significantly enhance the performance of large computers. The fastest speeds attained so far are only about ten trillionths of a second.

Recently, the U.S. Defense Department began developing plans for a new generation of supercomputers as part of an American effort to compete with Japan's Institute for New Generation Computer Technology, better known as Japan's fifth generation computer project. Japan's program, disclosed in October 1981, will concentrate heavily on AI technology and its use of knowledge rather than data. Research resulting from the American program is expected to have a tremendous impact on supercomputing technology. This research will focus on the development of a new generation of computers 10,000 times faster than present large computer systems.

The Japanese and some U.S. computer companies intend to reach extremely fast computer speeds by using what is called parallel processing—the simultaneous execution of many processes in the same computer. In fifth generation computers, thousands of processors will be used, all working together on the same problem, or even separate problems, at the same time. A great deal of research remains to be done in multiprocessing, but it is one of the latest advances in computer science.

AFTERWORD
GEE WHIZ,
BLUE SKY

Computer technology is advancing rapidly, and like it or not, computers will have a growing impact on all of us.

They will get smaller, but they will be able to do more things.

Like the silk weavers in Jacquard's time, some musicians are worried for their jobs as technology is getting to the point where the sound of an instrument (or an entire orchestra) can be contained on one computer chip.

Robots are being developed that can see to analyze images and perform inspection tasks in factories.

With specialized computers already available to help sailboats win races, other special computers for recreational activities are likely, such as hand-held navigational aids and communications gear for hikers.

Instead of having to carry keys, we will be identified by tiny computers which will scan the retinas of our eyes to identify us and automatically unlock doors.

We won't need coins for pay telephones. A computer will recognize our voices and add the pay phone calls to our home telephone bills.

In time, everyone will carry a "smart card" containing Social Security number, credit and health information, and a programmable personal identification code for use in bank automated-teller machines. The cards may also, when inserted into a special video machine, display our picture for positive identification purposes.

Rather than type letters or reports (for a homework assignment, for example), we will use voice-activated speech-to-text typewriters, or "talkwriters," which will translate sound waves of words into patterns to be identified by the computer's memory.

Even more fascinating, perhaps, is that the company that won an Academy Award for its computer-generated images of the planet Jupiter in the movie *2010* believes that at some point in the future re-creating actors may be possible. This would be done by "simulating" well-known actors from the past. Marilyn Monroe could star in a new movie with Harrison Ford. John Wayne could appear in a new Western thriller with Clint Eastwood.

The possibilities are endless, limited only by our imagination, and our ability to identify what people really need and want to make life easier and more productive.

FURTHER READING

Bits, Bytes, and Buzzwords. Hayward, CA: CompuPro Division of Godbout Electronics, 1983.

Moreau, R. *The Computer Comes of Age.* Cambridge, MA: MIT Press, 1984.

Richman, Ellen. *The Random House of Computer Literacy.* New York: Random House, 1982.

Rochester, Jack B., and Gantz, John. *The Naked Computer.* New York: William Morrow & Co., 1983.

INDEX